BALLADS OF A B

Ballads of a Bogman

Sigerson Clifford

MERCIER PRESS

MERCIER PRESS
PO Box 5, 5 French Church Street, Cork
and
16 Hume Street, Dublin 2

Trade enquiries to CMD DISTRIBIIflON
55a Spruce Avenve, Stillorgan Industrial Park, Blackrock, Dublin

A CIP record is arnilnble for this book from the British Library.

ISBN 1 85635010 X
First published in 1955, Mercier edition 1986.

10 9 8 7 6 5 4 3

Printed in Ireland by Colour Books Ltd.

Contents

To

Mary Anne Sigerson

and to Canburren Bog

in the morning

'0, Drink your Porter,
Tinker man'

0, Drink your porter, tinker man,
And wipe your creamy mouth,
The dust is white upon the roads,
The wind red from the south,
And where's the sense of footing fast
When your throat's on fire with drought?

Come, perch upon the barrel's edge
And slug the porter down,
We'll swop tales of the tinker men,
With women lean and brown,
Who sing the roads when old King Puck
Reigns in Killorglin town. . .

tinker: the Irish gipsy. Often a competent tinsmith but usually engaged
in the buying and selling of horses. mules and donkeys, It is held that the
tinkers are thedescendants of the Irish clans who supported James II. and
Who were, in consequence. dispossessed by William of Orange.

slug: from the Irish. To drink quickly.

King Puck: At the famous three-day fair held during August in Killor-
glin. County Kerry, a he-goat is crownedking, The origiDof the custom is
unknown.

The Ballad of the Tinker's Son

I was in school, 'twas the first of May,
The day the tinker came
With his wild wide eyes like a frightened hare's,
And his head with its thatch on flame.

We liked the length of his bare brown legs,
The patches upon his clothes,
The grimy strength of his unwashed hands
And the freckles about his nose.

The master polished his rimless specs
And he stared at him hard and long,
Then he stood him up on a shaky bench
And called on him for a song.

The tinker boy looked at our laughing lips,
Then with a voice like a timid bird's
He followed the master's bidding
And these are his singing words.

'My father was jailed for sheep-stealing,
My mother is black as a witch,
My sister off-ran with the Sheridan clan,
And my brother's dead-drunk in a ditch.

'0, Tralee jail would kill the devil,
But Tralee jail won't kill my da,
I'll mend yea kettle for one-and-fourpence
And bring home porter to my ma.'

He bowed his head as the schoolhouse shook
With the cheers of everyone,
Then the master made' me share my desk
With the raggedy tinker's son.

The days dragged by and he sat down there,
His brown eyes still afraid,
He heard the scholars' drowsy hum
And, turning to me, he said...

'Now what would I want with X and Y
And I singing the crooked towns,
Or showing a drunken farmer
The making of silver crowns?

'And will Euclid teach me to light a fire
Of green twigs in the rain,
Or how to twist a pheasant's neck
So it will not shout with pain?

'And what would I want with ancient verse
Or the meaning of Latin words
When all the poetry I'll ever need
Rings the throats of the singing birds?'

But he stayed at school and his flowering mind
Grew quick as a swooping hawk;
Then came a day when we said goodbye
To the master who smelt of chalk.

He went to the life' of ribbon roads
And the lore of the tinker bands;
They chained my bones to an office stool
And my soul to a clock's cold hands.

But I often thought of my tinker friend
And I cursed the smirking luck
That didn't make me a tinker man
Fighting the road to Puck.

With a red-haired wife and a piebald horse,
And a splendid caravan,
Roving the roads with Cartys and Wards,
The O'Briens or the Coffey clans.

The years went by and the Trouble came,
And I found myself again
Back where I whittled the worn desks,
With the mountains and the rain.

They put a trench-coat on my back,
And in my hands a gun,
And up in the hills with the fighting men
I found the tinker's son.

And there on the slopes of the Kerry hills
Our love grew still more strong,
And we watched the wrens on the yellow whins
Spill their thimblefuls of song.

Then came a truce and I shook his hand,
For a while our fighting done;
But I never spoke a word again
To the red-haired tinker's son ...

'Tis many a year since he went away
And over the roads the vans
Wheel gaily to horse and cattle fairs
With the O'Briens and the Coffey clans.

The tinker's son should be back again
With the roads and the life he knew,
But I put a bullet through his brain
In nineteen twenty-two.

The Trouble: the War of Independence.
Nineteen twenty-two: the Irish Civil War.

The Winkle Woman

O, but it is lonesome in Bolus by the sea,
No one on the cold strand but me and small Maggie
Searching round the hard rocks where the perries lurk,
In among the wet weeds, it's the weary work;
And the cold wind, the keen wind.
The wind would skin a Turk.

Fingers perished cruel, and sea waters ooze
Into tom stockings through our broken shoes.
Our poor backs are aching, paining us like mad,
Bent to pick the perries that's seldom to be had;
And Maggie, pale Maggie,
Maggie's coughing bad.

0, but it is killing to hear the wild waves roar
With himself lying there beneath them these five years or
more;
The cold wind blowing round us, booming like a drum,
And three children in the cabin and they hungry for a crumb,
So Maggie, pale Maggie,
Maggie had to come.

In the dusk of the evening I will hurry down
And sell my periwinkles in the cold strange town;
The people they will look at me, 'twill set them
wondering,
But with bread for the children
I'll be happier than a king;
Only Maggie, pale Maggie,
She'll never see the Spring.

The Ballad of the Tinker's Wife

When cocks curved throats for crowing
And cows in slumber kneeled,
She tiptoed out the half-door
And crossed her father's field.

Down the mountain shoulders
The ragged dawnlight came
And a cold wind from the westland
Blew out the last star's flame.

Her father, the strong farmer,
Had horses, sheep and cows,
One hundred verdant acres
And slates upon his house.

And she stole with the starlight
From where her life began
To roam the roads of Ireland
With a travelling tinker man.

His hair was brown and curling,
His eyes were brown as well,
His tongue would charm the hinges
Off the gates of hell.

At Caher fair she saw him
 As she was hurrying by,
And the song that he was singing
Would lure larks from the sky.

Her footsteps slowed to standing,
She stood and stared that day;
He made a noose of music
And pulled her heart away.

And so she left her slate-roof
And her father rich and strong
Because her mind was turning
About a tinker's song.

They walked the roads of Ireland,
Went up the hills and down,
Passed many an empty bogland,
Through many a noisy town.

She rode upon the ass-cart
To rest a tired leg,
She learned the lore of tinkers,
And he taught her how to beg.

'The tree-tied house of planter
Is colder than east wind,
The hall-door of the gombeen
Has no welcome for our kind.

'The farmstead of the grabber
Is hungry as a stone,
But the little homes of Kerry
Will give us half their own.'

She cut the cards for girls
And made their eyes glow bright;
She read the palms of women
And saw their lips go tight.

'A dark man will marry you
On a day of june;
There's money across water
Coming to you soon.

'0, he'll be rich and handsome
And I see a bridal feast;
Your daughter will dwell in Dublin,
Your son will be a priest.'

They rode along together,
The woman pale and wan,
The black ass young and giddy,
And the brown-eyed tinker man.

He bought up mules and jennets
And sang songs far and wide;
But she never gave him children
To fill his heart with pride.

She never gave him children
To spoil his sleep with cries,
But she saw his empty arms
And the hunger in his eyes.

She saw the lonely bogland,
She felt the killing wind,
And the fine home of her father
Kept turning in her mind.

She felt the chill rain falling,
She grew tired of it all,
And twisting in the darkness
She died within her shawl.

They dug a cold grave for her
And left her all alone,
And the tinker man went with them,
His heart as grey as stone.

'She was the best of women,
The flower of the ball,
She never gave me children
But that's no blame at all.

'A lass may break her mother's heart,
A son his father's head:
Maybe she is happier now
Sleeping with the dead.'

He drank his fill of porter
And turned his face to life,
And hit the road for Puck Fair
To get another wife.

planter: one of the landed gentry of English origin.
gombeen: an unscrupulous shopkeeper.
grabber: one who buys a farm from which the hereditary owners have
been evicted. A very unpopular person in Ireland.

I am Kerry

I am Kerry like my mother before me,
And my mother's mother and her man.
Now I sit on an office stool remembering,
And the memory of them like a fan
Soothes the embers into flame.
I am Kerry and proud of my name.

My heart is looped around the rutted hills
That shoulder the stars out of the sky,
And about the wasp-yellow fields
And the strands where the kelp-streamers lie;
Where, soft as lovers' Gaelic, the rain falls,
Sweeping into silver the lacy mountain walls.

My grandfather tended the turf fire
And, leaning backward into legend, spoke
Of doings old before quills inked history.
I saw dark heroes fighting in the smoke,
Diarmuid dead inside his Iveragh cave
And Deirdre caoining upon Naoise's grave.

I see the wise face now with its hundred wrinkles,
And every wrinkle held a thousand tales
Of Finn and Oscar and Conawn Maol,
And sea-proud Niall whose conquering sails,

Raiding France for slaves and wine,
Brought Patrick to mind Milchu's swine.

I should have put a noose about the throat of time
And choked the passing of the hobnailed years,
And stayed young always, shouting in the hills
Where life held only fairy fears.
When I was young my feet were bare
But I drove the cattle to the fair.

'Twas thus I lived, skin to skin with the earth,
Elbowed by the hills, drenched by the billows,
Watching the wild geese making black wedges
By Skelligs far west and Annascaul of the willows.
Their voices came on every little wind
Whispering across the half-door of the mind,
For always I am Kerry...

Diarmuid (pron. Dermot): with Finn. Oscar. Conawn Maol, Caoilte (pron, Keeltha) , Niall. Naoise (pron. Neesha), was one of the great fighting-men of pagan Ireland.

Iveragh: a barony in south Kerry.

Deirdre: the most beautiful woman in Irish legend. caoininy: Keening. wailing.

The Tinker's Wake

The pipes ringed crowns of smoke
About the angel's head
Who frowned from his painted frame
At the tinker stiff on the bed.

They waked him under the thatch,
Talking loud by the candle's flame,
He had died at Angelus-birth
And when he died they came.

Tinker men and their sons,
Shawled women bulky as bears,
They tiptoed over the threshold
And knelt to say their prayers.

He lay on the shaky bed
Nor knew when they crowded in,
His fingers cold on his beads,
A prayer-book under his chin.

They sat on the sugawn chairs
And the stools the neighbours brought,
We gave them porter to drink
And they prayed as they blew the froth.

'God's light be upon his soul,'
Their prayers were a bee's loud drone;
His ears were deaf to it all
And his lips were dry as a bone.

We gave them tobacco to smoke,
They puffed till the house went white,
Death's seals were over his eyes
And his, tongue and his teeth were tight.

We gave them dark-brown snuff,
'God's crown be on him,' they said.
Their prayers and sneezes were loud
But they could not wake the dead.

Last week his heart was young
And he knew the smell of the earth,
He closed no eye the night
The black ass moaned in birth.

He blew the froth from the pints
Of porter in Bawner's pub,
He sold the black ass's foal
And staggered home to his grub.

He knew the rain-washed moon,
The bell-breasted mountain rills,
And the grey skulls of the rocks
Half buried in the hills.

Many a head he cracked
In the rowdy fair of Puck,
Many a goose he stole
And many a plump-fed duck.

Many a salmon he poached,
But now he will poach no more;
The tinkers knelt and prayed
And went through the open door.

He lay in his stiff brown shroud
Nor knew when they went away,
And under the dying stars
A cock's throat called the day.

He stretched on the shaky bed
Nor knew when the day crept in,
His fingers blank on his beads,
A prayer-book under his chin.

sugawn chairs: chairs with seats made of rope.

The Fiddler

A black hat lumped on his skull,
A pipe stuck into his mouth,
His fingers fondled a fiddle
And his elbow jerked in and out.

His music was mad and merry,
I pranced like a circus clown,
He called me away and I followed
Him out of Cahirsiveen town.

The stars swam into the darkness
Cut by a curving moon,
The lamps made gold of the windows
As I followed the fiddler's tune

My mother peered out the half-door
And wept to see me pass;
I beckoned her follow the fiddler
And danced with him over the grass.

My father stood by the graveyard,
His eyes were bare of mirth,
Yet I knew my father was sleeping
In the heart of the Kerry earth.

Days and nights I followed
The fiddler who played to me,
And he fiddled me over the land,
And he fiddled me over the sea.

With never an hour for resting
Or sleep on a bed of sedge,
And after a moon of marching
We came to the world's edge.

And there the fiddler left me
While I wept and shouted his name,
And up in the sky the stars danced
On little shoes of flame.

The grey gulls mewed like kittens
As the curlews bubbled to sound,
The harps of the trees were wind-fingered
On the slopes of the higher ground.

A lapwing cried as it flew
Through a gap in the broken plough,
But the fiddler was gone for ever ...
And I am lonely now.

And my ears are dull from listening
For his voice upon the wind,
My eyes are dim from peering,
And there's madness in my mind.

I have grown grey with waiting
For him to come to me,
To fiddle me over the land
And to fiddle me over the sea.

The Ballad of the Tinker's Daughter

When rooks ripped home at eventide
And trees pegged shadows to the ground,
The tinkers came to Carhan bridge
And camped beside the Famine mound.

With long-eared ass and bony horse,
And blue-wheeled cart and caravan,
And she, the fairest of them all,
The daughter of the tinker clan.

The sun flamed in her red, red hair,
And in her eyes danced stars of mirth,
Her body held the willow's grace,
Her feet scarce touched the springing earth.

The night spread its star-tasselled shawls,
The river gossiped to its stones.
She sat beside the leaping fire
And sang the songs the tinker owns.

The songs as old as turning wheels
And sweet as bird-throats after rain,
Deep wisdom of the wild wet earth,
The pain of joy, the joy of pain.

A farmer going by the road
To tend his cattle in the byre
And saw her like some fairy queen
Between the river and the fire.

Her beauty stirred his brooding blood,
Her magic mounted in his head,
He stole her from her tinker clan
And on the morrow they were wed.

And when the sunlight swamped the hills
And bird-song drowned the river's bells,
The tinkers quenched their hazel fires
And climbed the windy road to Kells.

And from his house she watched them go
With blue-wheeled cart and caravan,
The long-eared ass and bony horse,
And brown-haired woman and tinker man.

She watched them go, she watched them fade
And vanish in the yellow furze:
A cold wind blew across the sun
And silenced all the singing birds.

She saw the months run on and on,
And heard the river fret and foam,
At white of day the roosters called,
At dim of dusk the cows came home.

The crickets strummed their heated harps
In hidden halls behind the hob
And told of distant waterways
Where the black moorhens dive and bob

And shoot the glassy bubbles up
To smash their windows on the stones;
And brown trout hide their spots of gold
Among the river's pebbly bones;

And, too, the. ebbing sea that flung
A net of sound about the stars
Set strange hills dancing in her dreams
And meshed her to the wandering cars.

She stole out from her sleeping man
And fled the fields that tied her down,
Her face moved towards the rising sun,
Her back was to the tired town.

She climbed the pallid road to Kells,
Against the hill, against the wind,
In Glenbeigh of the mountain-streams
She came among her tinker-kind.

They bedded her between the wheels
And there her son was born,
She heard the tinker-woman's praise
Before she died that morn ...

The years flew by like frightened birds
That spill a feather and are gone,
The farmer walked his weedful fields
And made the tinkers travel on.

No more they camped by Carhan bridge
And coaxed their fires to fragrant flame,
They saw him with his dog and gun,
They spat and cursed his name.

And when May hid the hawthorn trees
With stars she stole from out the skies
There came a barefoot tinker lad
With red, red hair and laughing eyes.

He left the road, he crossed the fields,
The farmer shot him in the side,
The smile went from his twisting lips,
He told his name and died.

That evening when the neighbours came
They found the son laid on the floor,
And saw the father swinging dead
Between the window and the door.

They placed the boy upon the cart
And cut the swaying farmer down,
They swear a tinker woman came
With them all the way to town.

The sun flamed in her red, red hair,
And in her eyes danced stars of mirth,
Her body held the willow's grace,
Her feet scarce touched the springing earth.

They buried them in Keelvarnogue
And eyes were moist and lips were wan,
And when the mound was patted down
The tinker maid was gone.

These things were long before my day,
I only speak with borrowed words,
But that is how the story goes
In Iveragh of the singing birds.

The Tale of the Tinker Man

Here's a health to you, Bard,
And there's slainte to me,
And may we both have thirsty throats
Till Ireland will be free.
And the bed we'll get in heaven
Let it be 'longside a pub;
Once eternity has liquor,
Hell the use we'll have for grub.

I was never a chap for trouble,
You might class me a man of peace,
If I ever saw fighting in the west
I went whistling to the east.
For a broken skull's no ornament
And bones are hard to mend,
And the big ashplant I carry,
Sure it only flogs the wind.

In Dingle town I met Kitchener
On a day I was five parts full,
And he gave me the silver shilling
To win the war for Bull.
I swopped my ashplant for a rifle,
Wrapped the puttees about my shins.
And clipped three years off Purgat'ry
In France for my liquid sins.

'Twas a queer hotel in the trenches,
Death paged us by day and dark,
For those wicked German snipers
Could shoot the eye from a lark.
But a lifetime of dodging peelers
Is training enough for a gom,
And devil the hole they drilled in me
With bullet, bayonet or bomb.

One day there came a regiment,
To beat a drum in the show,
And an English boy walked towards me
And smiled, and said hello.
Shining gold he was, and handsome
With his bandolier and gun;
Maybe he knew Greek and Latin
But he didn't know the Hun.

So I sat me down to teach him,
Praying he would not forget,
'Boy, don't you show an inch of hair
Above that parapet.'
The laughter crinkled up his lips
And wiped away the rule;
He like every beardless scholar
Thought his schoolmaster a fool.

I tiptoed towards the dugout.
At the door I turned around
As the boy fell like a broken branch

From the parapet to the ground.
He lay there silent on his back,
Staring at the skies,
And he never saw the round red hole
Between his blind blue eyes.

Well, here's a health to you, Bard,
And there's slainte to me,
And may we both have throats to cool
Till Ireland will be free.
And when we own four seas again
We'll right our country's wrongs;
Till then I'll drink your stout, Bard,
And you can sing my songs.

slcáinte: good health.
Kitchener: was born in North Kerry. Hence the tinker's name for the British recruiting-sergeant during the First World War.
gom: a dull-witted fellow.

The Boy Remembers His Father

The lips of laburnum drool fire,
Soon do the June days pass,
But always I'll remember
The swish of your feet through grass.

The swish of your feet through grass
And my bare toes at your side
When the sunlight left the sallies,
And the dancing mayflies died.

When the dancing mayflies died,
Their dance was merry and good,
You were a man and I was a boy
Walking through Carhan wood.

Walking through Carhan wood
While the field-mice sang in the hay,
And they cloaked their song in silence
When I ran to where they lay.

When I ran to where they lay
My bare feet noised like guns,
You laughed and called me away
With 'Don't frighten the timid ones.'

With 'Don't frighten the timid ones,'
And now you have frightened me;
I am always calling your name
Between the hill and the sea.

Between the hill and the sea
And through the quiet town;
They tell me they took you away
In a coffin of silver and brown.

In a coffin of silver and brown
While you lay lonely and still,
But I know you are hiding somewhere
Between the sea and the hill.

Between the sea and the hill
I'll hide in the lushy grass;
Where are you, 0 where are you?
I am waiting till you pass.

sallies: willows.

Brother Mick

The mountain frowned upon the school,
The school stared at the street,
And rich men's sons came there in shoes
While I ran in bare feet.
The rich had meat and cakes to eat,
And butter like the Danes,
While I had only spuds and fish,
And fish, they say, makes brains.
But still the rich boys passed exams
While I kept thin, and thick,
And thanked the stars that he had come
Among us... Brother Mick.

We had the world's slowest clock
That drowsed upon the wall
While I cursed the Roman scoundrels
That let Caesar loose in Gaul.
There, too, was Euclid with his cuts,
And trigonometry
That Peachy, Ring and Chas could do
But they were Greek to me.
And there were sums on trains and tubs
Of water running quick;
'Twas Chinese torture till he came
To save me ... Brother Mick.

For Brother Tom no patience had
With duffers such as I
Who never could be taught to solve
The mystery of pi.
And Brother Jim had even less
For those who didn't prize
The hairy men of hither Gaul
As seen through Caesar's eyes.
Then Brother Tom whacked like a bomb,
Well Jim could wield the stick,
But that was all before we knew
The smile of Brother Mick.

Still the great Power that will not let
The sparrow fall to earth
Took pity on bewildered brains
No Latin could alert.
For Brother Jim was sent to Trim
To march with Caesar there,
While we sprawled in our desks and heard
The new man on the stair.
We saw him smile as he came in,
His footsteps short and quick;
His name was Brother Michael
So, of course, we called him Mick.
And as the weeks meandered on
We watched with puzzled eye
And wondered if some archangel
Had strayed down from the sky.

He did not shout, he did not clout
But went his gentle way
To bring the light to souls that stood
Full ankle-deep in clay.
He locked the leather in the press
And burned the hazel stick;
'Twas then we all threw doubts upon
The mind of Brother Mick.

How short is time with one you love,
A year is like a while,
The things you will not do for stick
You learn for a smile.
We passed exams and scholarships,
Our mothers thought us fine,
Though greater than the loaves and fish
The miracle of mine.
The gods be praised I even got
Marks in arithmetic;
'You'll be a second Einstein yet,'
Said surprised Brother Mick.

The big lads reaped their excise jobs,
We all marched to the train
And shook their lordly hands and praised
The old school once again.
The engine panted up the rails,
We flung our cheers out loud
And watched it sprinting past the bridge,
Its whistle long and proud.

And as we laughed we little knew
The card Fate chose to pick,
How soon he'd be an exile, too,
Our splendid Brother Mick ...

The world has wheeled a lot since then,
Quiet are the hobs of home
And far from me these things are now
As is the moon from Rome.
But I can see the old school still
Stand tall above the street,
I smell the heather from the hill
And hear the running feet.
And in the door he walks again,
His footsteps short and quick,
And back across the years I wave
Goodbye to Brother Mick.

excise: the Kerry name for any and every civil service post.

Gubby Donovan's Pig

D' you know what I've been thinking and I sitting by the fire?
'Twas seventy winters from today I went to Cunnaclyre
With the pig for Gubby Donovan, who lived there west the
town
In a whitewashed little houseen that the years have crow-
barred down;
There's a bungalow in that spot now with roof like rusty wire,
Faith, names have changed an awful lot since the fair of Cun-
naclyre.

I was a supple blackguard then with neither pains nor aches,
And two swift naked heels by me as yellow as a drake's.
There was no garsoon near my age could jump me for a ball,
Or run a hundred spades with me, or clear a mountain-wall;
At sparring or at wrestling now 'tis I was tough to tire,
But I met my match the day I took the pig to Cunnaclyre.

I heard it on the listening-in only the other night
To feed bananas to the pigs if you wanted them all right.
We hadn't bananas for ourselves. nor oranges nor date,
But yellow meal and coshawawn we gave the beast to ate;
And Gubby hadn't yellow meal but nettles barbed like wire,
Small blame he was the leanest pig that e'er saw Cunnaclyre

He was as nimble as a bee and hardy as a flail,
You'd swear he was a greyhound with a corkscrew in his tail,
He leaped the big spiked railway gate as easy as a bet
And Gubby cried, 'Allana now, go gentle with the pet.'
The snuff from out the mustard-box she sniffed it like a fire,
But 'twas I that did the sneezing on the road to Cunnaclyre.

He galloped down the village street, his two tusks dripping
foam,
He cleared the roads like Hannibal the time he marched on
Rome,
He drove the cats up to the roofs and the terriers to the wood,

He closed the pubs far quicker than the sergeant ever could;
And Tom' the Bell, our parish clerk, took refuge in the spire
As I tried to coax that atheist on the road to Cunnaclyre.
Then off he dashed for open ground as fast as he could flake,
He crossed two rivers, twenty streams, a cummer and a lake;
He trotted over Beenatee, a hill of no small fame,
But if it was Mount Everest he'd scale it just the same.
Signs by, the veins upon his back stood out like fencing wire
And the jobbers told us what to do with him at Cunnaclyre.

He wandered wild about the place a few years after then
Till we trapped him for a circus-man who kept a tiger's den.
We mourned his going a little while and soon the news came
round
That he killed and ate a tiger who was worth a hundred pound.
They shot him then at Scartaglin and there he did expire,
Far, far away from all his friends and the fields of Cunnaclyre.

garsoon: a young lad.

a hundred spades: a spade is five feet, i.e. the approximate length of the implement itself.

coshawawn: Irish name for the dandelion.

cummer: from the Irish. A ravine.

signs by: as a result.

The Circus

It was Patie Doyle that saw it first,
As out of school in a wave we burst,
The poster coloured and gay;
We crowded round and our eyes grew wide,
We fought tooth and claw to get inside
And read of the Great O'Shay.
We piped our glee like a flock of birds
As the promises of the painted words
Thrilled us up and down.
In one short week, and it seemed a year,
The great O'Shay would be striding here,
The circus was coming to town.

And Bongo, the clown, all red and white,
The crowned heads of Europe hailed with delight
There were crowns in Europe then -
Would sing his songs and make us laugh,
And nowhere the beating of Biggerstaffe,
The prince of the slack-wire men.
The troupe of monkeys, the kangaroo,
The mule that could count to thirty-two,
And the dog that jumped through a hoop!
Well, the perjuring posters swore their lies
In coloured oaths of tremendous size
And we swallowed them line and loop.

The circus came and took its stand
In a field of Johnny Casey's land
And in hundreds we crowded in;
The young in front and the old behind,
And the middle the men of substance lined
Tight as beans in a tin.
We sat by the ring with our hearts agog,
Counted by the eyes of O'Shay's dog,
Waiting for the band to play,
But the only tunes were the rasping moans
Of the corncrakes with their saxophones
In Mike MacCarthy's hay.

Then O'Shay with beard like flaming gorse
Leaped on and off a spavined horse,
And groaned when he hit the ground;
But the wonder was he could jump at all,
For his boots were as long as the China Wall,
And he weighed two hundred pound.
So we clapped his jumps and we cheered his groans
As the great man lifted his mighty bones,
And we thought him the best alive.
And he smiled at us with crimson gums
When the counting mule who was good at sums
Said two and two make five.

He chanted the ballad of Fontenoy,
He sang us the 'Bonnie Labouring Boy'
In a shout that would drown a band.
With three white plates he juggled around

And Pete Murphy cried when one struck the ground,
'May God give you another hand.'
He planted his voice in a timber man,
He hid pigeons' eggs in a gallon can
And they hatched out rabbits nine.
He grinned and swallowed a sword of steel,
He did more turns than the conger-eel
That ate a porcupine.

With never a sign of Biggerstaffe
Or the clown that made the crowned heads laugh,
Or the boxing kangaroo;
And the troupe of monkeys had shrunk in size
To one little mite with wistful eyes
Tied up in a coat of blue.
Our hearts grew hard and we clapped no more
As the big man pranced on the circus floor,
Or fumbled with bits of delf;
For it hit us clear as the light of day
That the calvalcade of the Great O'Shay
Was the Great O'Shay himself.

As he smiled at us through his beard of gold
We thought of the lies the posters told
And our anger rose in a flood;
And the lads who ducked in through a canvas crack
Began to demand their money back
And shouted for O'Shay's blood.
But with head held high he stood his ground

As the seats snapped loudly all around,
And he spat in the gallon can;
And he showed his teeth in a fighting way
Till a sod that was meant for the Great O'Shay
Knocked the head off the timber man.

But some nervous gom for the police had sent
And they came at a trot and cleared the tent,
And whistled us into the night.
We galloped home beneath freckled skies
Past the perjuring posters, red with lies,
Which we tore to make things right.
And we wondered if we ever would
See circuses that were near as good
As the posters swear they are.
But growing old makes the half-fool wise
And 'tis only now I realise
That O'Shay's was better by far.

The Ballad of Lascar Rock

The lighthouse upon Lascar Rock
Stands like a whitened bone,
As lonely as a guillemot
Upon a seawashed stone,
And in the house on Lascar Rock
I tended the light alone.

The lantern into the sky
Its yellow warning flings,
And in that dark star-empty sky
Where never a bird-voice sings
The wild geese fly and I can hear
The whistling of their wings

The grey gulls feed their scrawny young
Upon the rock's foul side,
The gannets peer with evil eyes
Above the lurching tide;
They seem to tell me that they know
It was my son who died.

The clouds were crowding up the west
When he sailed from the town,
And when he came by Lascar Rock
The storm-rains lashed down,

And terrible it was to stand
And watch my own son drown.

The thunder crashed about the heels
Of the searchlight from the skies
That lit the broken boat and showed
The terror in his eyes.
The crabs that crawl round Lascar Rock
Will tell you where he lies.

Weeks passed, I mourned my missing son
While the catlike waters purred;
One day I heard a little sound
Just like a muttered word,
I looked and saw the bomber-plane
No bigger than a bird.

I watched it big and bigger grow
Above the level sea,
Its humming nose and heavy wings
Like some gigantic bee;
It came down low by Lascar Rock
And hands waved out at me.

Across the shoulders of the tide
I saw its arrowed flight
And when the mists hung from the stars
And the gulls screamed in the night,
It dipped and made a circle once
Around the Lascar light.

Above the cold weed-tangled stones
The ebb tide curves and runs,
Throughout the weeks they waved to me
From their war-world of guns;
I watched the light on Lascar Rock
And dreamed they were my sons.

My one son drowned within the sea,
My four sons in the sky,
I knelt all night on Lascar Rock
And prayed they would not die:
The lantern circled in the dark
And flashed *They shall not die.*

The storm-wind whipped from the west,
Seas lashed my rocky moat,
And somewhere in the tortured air
I heard the engine's note
Like the broken gasping sound that comes
From a dying sea-pig's throat.

The wind cracked like a thousand whips,
And waves leaped lantern-high,
And as I prayed I heard the plane
Come crashing from the sky:
It was so dark I could not see
My other four sons die.

I cannot close my tired eyes
But I see them all again,

My one son in the broken boat,
My four sons in the plane:
They look at me with eyes that hurt
My poor bewildered brain.

I sit beside the fire at night
Where no small cricket sings
And up against the lantern-glass
I hear their beating wings,
Like tired swallows coming home
From Egypt of the Kings.

When midnight spans the heaving tide
The dead walk three and four
From out their weed-red rocky tombs
Upon the dim sea-floor:
With fearful eyes I watch the dead
March past the lighthouse door.

I rush across the darkened Rock
To leave this haunted place,
The grey gulls scream, the gannets shriek
And peer into my face:
O God above, the awful birds
Smash wings against my face. . .

When they sailed out to Lascar Rock
They found him sitting there,
A childish grin upon his lips
And seaweed on his hair,

And he kept looking at the sea
With an unwinking stare.

He came down like a timid child,
He sat within the boat,
And they climbed up the lighthouse stair
And left him there afloat:
With whitened beard and moving jaws
He looked so like a goat.

He looked so very like a goat,
They left him there alone
And when they reached the lighthouse door
They heard a little moan,
And saw him dive into the sea
And sink down like a stone.

They searched but never found a trace
Till darkness dimmed their eyes
And the lighthouse flung its yellow spears
Of warning through the skies.
The crabs that crawl round Lascar Rock
Know full well where he lies.

Country Pub

When wind harped on strings of rain
And the stars were mackerel-cold,
I came to the crossroads pub
And the glow of its windowed gold.

A house half-thatch, half-slate
Where a lamp in the corner kneels,
And the red bellies of the porter barrels
Make floors for jigging heels.

An old man curved like a bow
Scraped nails on the flagged stones
And with thimble of amber fire
Stitched heat to his brittle bones.

Saying, 'Down by the dunes of Trawbawn
When dawn peeled the sands of night
Ossian came galloping over the sea
Pauper-hungry for fight .

'And how was the Playboy to know
That shillelagh was splintered by bell,
And Ireland sack-empty of fight
Since Finn went froglepping to hell?

'Oscar. Caoilte, Con awn
And Diarmuid, damned for they sinned
In worshipping Baal and Crom,
All gone like a Druid wind.

'They were the men of steel
Who swung the sword and the flail:
And they're tacked to the rafters of hell
By Beelzebub's red-hot nail.

'D'ye think if they came back now,
Those men of the warrior bone,
That our fourth green field would be
A rag tied to an alien throne?

'Ah, Ireland is only a ruin,
A patch on a gombeen's coat.'
The old man splintered his glass
And growled in his martial throat.

The door let in the starlight
And startled the oil-lamp's flame,
The old man went and we questioned
But no one knew his name.

Each man flung a mighty shadow
As each nursed his little grief.
I ran outside to the gable
But the roads were bare as a leaf.

Down by the sea's dim margin
Something mysterious stirred,
A coloured cloak half seen,
The neigh of a horse half heard.

They went and the water troubled
The night with its rolling cars,
And up in the skyey meadows
Pranced a riderless horse of stars.

Baal and Crom: the pagan gods of Ireland.

fourth green field: The six north-eastern counties of Ireland. There is a
tradition that the pagan hero, Ossian, returned from the Land of Youth
to see how Ireland was faring. He was warned not to let his foot touch
the ground, but his horse's saddle slipped and he fell. He had a talk with
Saint Patrick before he died.

The Races

'Twas a day in September that I'll always remember,
I went with my father to Carhan's old school
And there on the racecourse were gathered in great force
Rich man and poor man, wild boy and tame fool.
There were tinkers from Galway as brown as a ha'penny,
A beggar with whiskers the longest I've seen,
The three-card-trick Johnny and the four-shots-a-penny
On the day of the races in Cahirsiveen.

'Twas a rich Tower of Babel beside the school gable
Where the bookies were shouting and laying the odds,
'Twould take Atlas so hairy or our own Steve Casey
To win through the crowds packed like peas in their pods.
There were tents like umbrellas where all kinds of fellows
Sold dilisc and shellfish and the juicy crubeen,
And penny Peg's legs the size of a peeler
On the day of the races in Cahirsiveen,

The jockeys they sat on their horses like statues,
Their fame will remain while the Fertha shall flow:
'Tis my hero, Padgen, I'd pin a bright badge on,
With the two gallant Griffins, Jimmie and Johnjoe.
Denis Donovan, too, from high Bawr na Srawde,
And Courtney, Saint Brendan's, were sporting and keen,
While Jack Rock's spurs a-jingle would make your blood tingle
On the day of the races in Cahirsiveen.

The horses, God bless them, in dreams I caress them,
The wild-things of beauty stole the heart from my side,
As I watched them fly over the grass and red clover
And sweep like the wind east by Reenrusheen tide.
They skimmed the hawbushes, they dashed through the rushes,
Their jockeys arrayed in blue, scarlet, and green:
'Twas the world's eighth wonder to hear their hooves thunder
On the day of the races in Cahirsiveen.

O that night men did gather, hearts light like a feather.
Round a meegum in Bawner's or a pint at the Plow,
They toasted the horses that won out their courses
And shouted their praises while time did allow.
'Here's a health to you, Terry, and O'Neill's Pride of Kerry,

Likewise Lass from Sussa, the westland's swift queen:
May ye graze in high heaven and have comfort for ever,
Ye're the pride of the races in Cahirsiveen.'

My father is gone now, God's peace to his ashes,
The boys are young men and the old men are dead,
There is many a mile between me and the racecourse,
But the hooves of the horses beat loud in my head.
I give you my oath now I'd swop the wide world
To call back the bright days when proud I had been
A lad with his dad on the white road to Carhan,
And the splendid horse-races in Cahirsiveen.

Steve Casey: a Kerryman who became a world champion at
wrestling.
dilisc: edible seaweed.
crubeen: a pig's trotter.
Peg's legs: brown-coloured sugar-sticks.
Fertha: a river in South Kerry.
meegum: from 'medium'. A measure varying from a half-pint to a pint
but nearer to a pint.

The Ballad of the Tinker's Christmas

'Tis a tale the tinkers told me and we camped beside the bridge
Where the oaks of Hillgrove beckon to the stars,
And the brown owl on the old mill gave his banshee wail again,
And the wood fire thumbed its shadows on the cars.

I sat there watching upwards where the Tinsmith of the tribes
Scattered stars and crescent moon about the sky,
And the pieces, white like silver, glistened with eternal dews
As His scissors shaped the dipper with a craftsman's steady eye.

Shawn Gow, the blacksmith, ruled the forge beside the hazel
wood
Where four roads meet and mingle like old friends come from
afar,
And when he saw the tinker men sweep past the smithy door
The hate blinked from his dusty eyes as light winks from a star.

For Gow, the smith, walked with a maid when April was
abroad
And she promised that she'd wed him when the trees had lost
their green;
But Tammy Brien, the tinker king, came laughing down the
road
And when the summer fled the fields she reigned the tinker's
queen.

The smith should be the friend of men who take the road for
mate
For with iron that the blacksmith beats are tinkerhorses shod;
And he who hates the tinker men should make no boast of
hate
For the stick the tinker carries is from ash tree grown by God.

The bellows hissed into the coals, the iron: glowed to red,
The blacksmith picked his hammer up and made the anvil ring;
A shadow fell across the sparks that danced about his head
And, looking up, the blacksmith saw the smiling tinker king.

'Away from this place, tinker man, I'll pare no hoof for you,

And take the road to the next forge while yet your road is good;
No shoe I'll shape for men who made the three hard iron nails
For Him who died between two thieves upon a cross of wood.'

The smile drained from the tinker's eyes like sunlight from a
pool
When the cloud-sheep seek their pastures on the blue skies'
airy trails;
A liar was your father, Gow; your mother reared a fool,
Twas the blacksmith blew the bellows and the blacksmith
forged the nails.'

Then face to face they glared their hate within the smithy
smoke,
The tinker man light as a cat, the smith broad like a bull;
The muscled arm swept aloft, the hammer swung and missed,
And the ashplant cracked its leaden butt into the blacksmith's
skull.

O there are men who love the wind and men who like the rain,
And men who'll hate the roof of slate until the hour they die;
The white road ribbons through their dreams and

turns and calls again.
And not for them the prison cell and the barred patch of sky.

Five years can build an army up to burn and waste and slay,
And five can tear a city down that's higher than the stars;
Five years can take the mind of man and shape it to "rich clay,
What five can make five, too, can break behind the prison bars.

The big gates closed behind the king, the gray fog hugged the
street,
And muffled by the lowered sky the city's sullen roar;
His home was south, he hurried west on quick impatient feet,
He travelled one, he spoke to none, and sought his tribe no
more.

He built his fire beside a stream when Christmans blessed the
hills,
His company the brown owl's hoot, the raven's friendless croak;
The patter of the donkey's hoofs came towards him from the
east,
A bearded man who bore a staff, a woman in a cloak.

He gave them bread as there they talked beside the leaping fire,
The knots that bruised his tired brain unravelled one by one;
'Now do you know if long ago 'twas smith or tinker man
That forged the nails for Him who died against the eastern sun?'

All wistful grew the woman's eyes: 'Not smith nor tinker rude,
But he who wrongs the widow's child that is by angels blest,
Who sends away with empty hands the poor man to his brood,
He made the nails for Him who sleeps in peace against my breast.'

The tinker 'King' is always a good fighter. It is an Irish tradition that the Holy Family travel the roads of the world again. with an understand-able preference for the roads of Ireland. each Christmas. Hence the beautiful Irish custom of placing a lighted candle in the window of every house in rural parts. and leaving the doors unlocked in case they call to rest a while.

The Kerry Christmas Carol

Brush the floor and clean the hearth,
And set the fire to keep,
For they might visit us tonight
When all the world's asleep.

Don't blow the tall white candle out
But leave it burning bright,
So that they'll know they're welcome here
This holy Christmas night.

Leave out the bread and meat for them,
And sweet milk for the Child,
And they will bless the fire that baked
And, too, the hands that toiled.

For Joseph will be travel-tired,
And Mary pale and wan,
And they can sleep a little while
Before they journey on.

They will be weary of the roads,
And rest will comfort them,
For it must be many a lonely mile
From here to Bethlehem.

O long the road they have to go,
The bad mile with the good,
Till the journey ends on Calvary
  Beneath a Cross of wood.

Leave the door upon the latch,
And set the fire to keep,
And pray they'll rest with us tonight
When all the world's asleep.

Lenihan's Big Bazaar

They've pictures in the village now, the ones that talk for
hours
The greatest kind of rawmaish since they built the Babel
towers;
And sometimes they're in colours for to make their meaning
plain.
And unless I'm gone contrairy they rank Abel less than Cain.
You'd get a brown taste in your mouth to see the carry-on,
With their kissing and their cuddling until half the night is
gone.
They've a gentleman with wavy hair, he's what they call a
Star;
Faith, he wouldn't light the sky for long in Lenihan's Big
Bazaar.

We had simple ways to pass the days in our village on the
hill,
The football, and the baigles, and the dancing by the Mill.
The night-time was the worst of all, the hours dragged slow
and lame,
The great diversion that we had was when the Missioners
came;

We were only middling sinners with little venials to our score.
So they blessed our beads and left us and the night flowed back
once more.
We talked and yawned and went to bed till, eastward by Glen-
car,
We saw the lights that marked the vans of Lenihan's Big Ba-
zaar.

Then, boys o' war, the world wheeled bright around the Market
House
With the roulette and the rocky-boats and the game of cat and
mouse;
And the wheel of fortune shining like a rainbow in the sky.
With gold too at the end of it for them that paid to try.
Twas fun to aim the shooting gun at the dainty dancing ball,
Or to gamble for the trophies in the lovely chaney stall.
Faith, yesterday the pensions-man came in his motor-car
And he took a sup out of a cup I won in the Bazaar.

And then the concert on the stage, the fiddle and the fife.
The dancing and reciting, and the sketches drawn from life.
We walked the hard road with Parnell, we died in jail with
Tone.

And we cheered the men who sketched them, Shawn O'Grady
and Malone.
I hear praise on the listening-in for this and that boyo;
Sure, they wouldn't hold a candle to Tom Storey long ago.
With the clawhammer and battered boots, the cane and the
cigar,
He roofed the sky with smiles for slates in Lenihan's Big Ba-
zaar.

'Twould do you good to hear the tunes that knocked sparks
from the eye,
And the fine old all-for-Ireland songs that had no right to die.
The brothers, Matt and Christy, were the best the world has
seen
And we loved them as we heard them pay their tribute to the
Green;
Not like the trash they're singing now, a kind of banshee's
moan,
And you wouldn't hear them drool at all without that micro-
phone.
There's Patsy Ryan had but one lung, and that one bore a scar,
And you'd hear him up in Driscoll's wood from Lenihan's Big
Bazaar.

And Kathleen O'Reilly now, 'tis she had steps galore
In those shining dawny shoes of hers the times she took the
floor;
The Blackbird and the Rayhill reel she danced them like a joy
And tripped her way into the heart of one small watching boy.
O she was young and I was young, and life was good and sweet,
And all my dreams were spancelled to her little twinkling feet;
I wondered would she stick the land but my hopes smashed
like a jar
When I saw her smile at Boxty Walsh in Lenihan's Big Bazaar.

Well, they've pictures in the village now and may they do it
good;
They've swapped Kilmichael and Clontarf for this place called
Hollywood.
There's grass growing green around the Mill where we danced
the Kerry Set
While they're trotting down a jazz-hall through a bog of dust
and sweat.
They're changing days and altered nights, but still shines like a
star
The kindly glow of lights long quenched in Lenihan's Big
Bazaar.

Bazaar: a travelling, open-air show. The talkies killed the most of them. unfortunately.

Kilmichael and Clontarf: We won a gun-argument with the Sassanach in the former place. and a sword-and-battleaxe bout with the Danes in the latter.

Clawhammer: old-fashioned coat with tails to it.

The Ghost Train for Croke Park

I'm living here in London not as young then as I was,
And the poor skull neatly tonsured at the top
And the crow's feet at the corners kicking strongly for my ears,
I'll be lucky if 'tis at my ears they stop.
But this London that I mentioned, though 'tis fair enough by
day,
Can be lonely as a fiddle after dark;
Ah, old town beneath the mountain, 'tisn't poor I was but rich
On the night we took the ghost train for Croke Park.

Wisha, God be with you, Kerry, where they never lock the fire,
With the kettle singing on the sooty crane,
And my mother - 'Will you hurry now and leave the mirror
sound,
Myko Lairy's passing Hurley's with the train.'
Then the quick run out the half-door of that houseen down the
lane,
And I dressed as neat as any Excise clerk
With the blue suit and the brown boots and the medal on its
chain.
The night we took the ghost train for Croke Park.

Ah, I mind it all so clearly when the stars danced on the hills
With their faces scrubbed and shiny, and the powder in their
hair,
And the tide across the sandbanks turning lazy in its sleep,
And a lonesome curlew, bubbling here and there.
We all met at Keating's corner when 'twas midnight by the
clock -
Casey's mouth-organ made music like a lark
And we gave the Kerry war-cry as we marched north two by
two
To lep aboard the ghost train for Croke Park.

And the ree-raw at the station, faith, 'twas better than Puck
Fair
With the shouldering, and shouting, and the din;
We had bottles full of lemonade, and biscuits, for the boys,
And 'a brew beagawneen stronger for the men.
Dan Keeffe blew on his whistler and he waved the green flag
high,
Beyond by Foxy Jack's place I could hear a shepherd bark,
And we shouted 'Goal for Kerry!' at the inoffending sky
As the ghost train left the station for Croke Park.

We spread a coat between us and we handed out the cards,

Sure we always brought the deck for thirty-wan,
But 'tis talk we did, not gamble, for with football in our brain
The card-game closed as soon as it began.
'Twas Kildare that we were playing, and we gave them little chance,
As the cards lay face-down, idle on our laps,
And 'twas Kerry, Kerry, Kerry while the stars kept up their dance;
All you'd see on the Kildare side was our caps.

Bob Doyle, who knew his football, swore that we'd win by a goal,
The Tailor felt we'd get there by a street,
And myself, may God forgive me, thought by twenty points or so,
'Wisha, five or six is plenty,' said John Pete.
'Their backs will never hold us if they lepped up to the moon,'
And Dave Hanley nodded wisely at Pat Clarke.
All the experts had the scoreboard chalked up ere the ball was thrown,
In the ghost train steaming proudly for Croke Park.

Then the soft grass and the sunshine and the marching of the bands,
With the green and gold flag fluttering over all,
There's Con Brosnan running swiftly and our Sheehy shooting low,
And Larry Stanley jumping skyhigh for the ball.

It put the heart across me when the leather grazed our goal,
And my throat with shouting tattered like a scraw;
There was never sweeter music than that final whistle blown,
And the board said, let me whisper, 'twas a draw.

Loud and long we held the inquest steaming home from Dub-
lin town,
And we wrote down who kicked well and who played poor,
But John Pete agreed with me that all the luck was with Kil-
dare,
And Bob Doyle maintained we'd win the next time sure.
We still chalked up the scoreboard, and the chalk was green
and gold;
Said the Tailor, white teeth grinning like a shark,
'Sure, we only took their measure and we'll cut the doth to
scale
When we take the Ghost Train three weeks for Croke Park.'

Trains left the more distant parts of Ireland on midnights Saturday
for the Gaelic, Football Cup Final in Dublin, Sunday. Kerry and County
Kildare were popular rivals. Three points (over the aossbarbut between
the extended posts) equal-one goal. Kerry's jersey is green and gold.

Kerry's Footballers

Plough and spade and seineboat shaped them for the deeds
they were to do,
Street and school and mountain heard their victory -cry.
Now their memories arch like rainbows o'er the meadows' of
the mind,
The Alive who'll live for ever, and the Dead who'll never die.

When the stranger came steel-fisted and the hounds bayed in
the glen,
0, my Kingdom of the half-doors and the white wet window-
sills,
Where the gun-smoke wrote its message there the great foot-
balling men
Fought the flame-red rearguard battle of the hills.

0, the gold bells of the old days tinkle wistful in my mind
And I see the fireman dark against the light,
Hear the whistle whimper lonely o'er the dead leaves of the
years
As the ghost train races swiftly through the night.

These the men your fathers spoke of in the game your fathers loved,
These the men who blazed the trail and made it fair ...
In my dreaming now I see them as I saw them long ago,
Green and gold, and white limbs leaping when our Kerry played Kildare ...

The County Mayo
(*After the Irish of Raftery*)

Now spring is primrosing the hazel woods again,
And the days are stretching a cockstep or so,
After the feast of Breeda I'll hoist my sail for the
west,
And devil the anchor I'll drop till I come to the county Mayo.

Under thatch in Claremorris I'll snuggle the first
night,
In the tavern beyond it I'll rent a spitoon;
The priest of Kiltimagh I'll hear for four Sundays,
Then for Ballinamore will I trim my balloon.

My wings work as fast as a cuckoo's godmother,
Or a droileen's widow with a score of young,
When I think of the nights with the glasses brimming
I'll spend in the ale-house my friends among.

Song and dance and the ball of laughter
Will bounce and roll on the sanded floor;
Were I there now where the yarns are spinning
Youth would come on me and I'd be old no more.

Feast of Breeda: Saint Brigid's Day.
Droileen: wren.
Raftery: a blind and restless poet of Connacht.

Roger Casement

O let them rake their muck now and pile it Brandon- high,
And grind the bones to powder and spill it on the land;
Enough for us a tall man came with salt spray on his beard,
And smiled to see the ropes of weed on lonely Banna Strand.

O let them fling their stones now nor heed the splintering
glass;
I drained a dram with Monteith and he took me by the hand,
And he told me of the tall man with the green flag in his
mind
Who rose from out the noose of sea on lonely Banna Strand.

The tall man in McKenna's Fort saw the dark upon the hills;
He touched his lantern to a star and lighted up the land.
Enough for us the blinds are drawn and crepe is on the door,

Enough we slept while Casement wept on lonely Banna
Strand.

Brandon: a mountain in west Kerry.
Monteith: came in the submarine with Casement. His escape from
Banna makes exciting reading.

The Old School

That was a gay place they planted your feet, Old School,
With your windows beckoning the mountains in,
So we could watch the hawk's wings nailed to the sky
While the linnet sang on the whin.
Hard on the eye the old books in the summer weather,
And then Master and hawk swooping out of the blue sky
together.

That was a grey day I said goodbye, Old School,
And you wiped the chalk from your hand and wished me joy.
Searching ever the mind moves down the dust of the years
To see in the lively playground the ghost of a laughing boy.
Lingers the longing always for Youth's green sunlit tracks
Now the harsh old world has broken its cane on our backs.

M. J. MacManus

I remember how his hand reached out for mine
When youth was a spancel tying me to the hills.
Tradition was a cool spring-well under hazels.
He bade me drink deep and listen
To the green branches growing.

I urged my shadow before me across furze-squared grasses,
And heard bog-water telling its amber beads over pebbles.
Knowing tomorrow I'd give him today's speckled wonders
I cherished the brown bird of contentment
By some travelling tinker's fire,

Now the hills wade through silence and bare the hob-corners
Where the old men thatched their dreams with adjectives.
Some day, maybe, on our bones they will build sky-scrapers.
Still green grow the restless rushes
In the meadows of the mind. . .

Francis Ledwidge

I think of you when over Primrose Wood
The rooks fly wing on wing to raid the oats,
And cuckoos on the warm exploding furze
Announce their presence from vainglorious throats.

You are the boy that runs through Driscoll's fields
When morning's dew revives the pale Woodbines,
Your bare feet crushing to the cooling leaves
The gold testudo of the dandelions.

And from the fence where fox-gloves fish the bees,
When June's red current flames the streams of air,
I see you bending over Griffin's well
The dust of summer in your dreaming hair.

Is this our Eden where two robins make
A semi-colon on a page of snow?
Is there more music in the blackbird's flute
Than Death will ever show?

The Boys of Barr na Sraide

O the town it climbs the mountain and looks upon the sea,
And sleeping time or waking 'tis there I long to be,
To walk again that kindly street, the place I grew a man
And the Boys of Barr na Sraide went hunting for the wran.

With cudgels stout we roamed about to hunt the droileen
We looked for birds in every furze from Letter to Dooneen:
We sang for joy beneath the sky, life held no print or plan
And we Boys in Barr na Sraide, hunting for the wran.

And when the hills were bleeding and the rifles were aflame,
To 'the rebel homes of Kerry the Saxon stranger came,
But the men who dared the Auxies and beat the Black and Tan
Were the Boys of Barr na Sraide hunting for the wran.

And here's a toast to them tonight, the lads who laughed with me,
By the groves of Carhan river or the slopes of Beenatee,
John Dawley and Batt Andy, and the Sheehans Con and Dan,
And the Boys of Barr na Sraide who hunted for the wran.

And now they toil on foreign soil, where they have gone their way
Deep in the heart of London town or over in Broadway.
And I am left to sing their deeds, and praise them while I can
Those Boys of Barr na Sraide who hunted for the wran.

And when the wheel of life runs down and peace comes over me,
O lay me down in that old town between the hills and sea,
I'll take my sleep in those green fields the place my life began,
Where the Boys of Barr na Sraide went hunting for the wran.

MORE INTERESTING BOOKS

THE RED-HAIRED WOMAN
AND OTHER STORIES

'He blamed Red Ellie for his failure to sell. She stood before him on the road that morning, shook her splendid mane of foxy hair at him, and laughed. He should have returned to his house straightaway and waited 'till she left the road. It was what the fishermen always did when they met her. It meant bad luck to meet a red-haired woman when you went fishing or selling. Everyone knew that .. :

'This collection of stories has humour, shrewd observation, sharp wit at times, and the calm sure touch of an accomplished storyteller ...'
From the Introduction by Brendan Kennelly

Each of 'Sigerson Gifford's delicious tales ... in *The Red-Haired Woman and Other Stories* is a quick, often profound glimpse of Irish life, mostly in the countryside. The characters appear, fall into a bit of trouble and get wherever they're going without a lot of palaver. The simple plots glisten with semi-precious gems of language ...'
James F. Clarity, The New York Times Book Review

'Flavoured by the wit and sweetness of the Irish language, this slender volume presents brief affectionate glimpses of Irish country life.'
Leone McDermott, Booklist

GEMS OF IRISH WISDOM :
Irish Proverbs and Sayings
Padraic O'Farrell

Gems of Irish Wisdom is a fascinating collection of Irish proverbs and sayings.

The tallest flowers hide the strongest nettles.

The man who asks what good is money has already paid for his plot.

A man begins cutting his wisdom teeth the first time he bites off more than he can chew.

Even if you are on the right track, you 11 be run over if you stay there.

The road to Heaven is well sign posted but badly lit at night. Love is like stirabout, it must be made fresh every day.

The begrudger is as important a part of Irish life as the muck he throws.

Love at first sight often happens in the twilight.

The man who hugs the altar-rails doesn't always hug his own wife.

If a man fools me once, shame on him. If he fools me twice shame on me.

God never closes one door but He opens another.

Hating a man doesn't hurt him half as much as ignoring him.

Every cock crows on his own dunghill.

A kind word never gets a man into trouble.

IN MY FATHER'S TIME
Eamon Kelly

In My Father's Time invites us to a night of storytelling by Ireland's greatest and best loved *seanchaí*, Eamon Kelly. The fascinating stories reveal many aspects of Irish life and character. There are tales of country customs; matchmaking, courting, love; marriage and the dowry system; emigration. American wakes and returned emigrants. The stream of anecdotes never runs dry and the humour sparkles and illuminates the stories.

Nowadays we find it hard to visualise the long dark evenings of times gone by when there was no electric light, radio or T.V. We find it even harder to realise that such evenings were not long enough for the games, singing, music, dancing and storytelling that went on.

In My Father's Time is based on Eamon Kelly's successful one man show. It was first presented by the Abbey Theatre at the Peacock in June 1975 and it was equally successful on its tour of Ireland's chief towns and cities.

Lightning Source UK Ltd.
Milton Keynes UK
UKOW04f0728311017

311934UK00001B/85/P